THE GREAT MEDIEVAL YELLOWS

EMILY WILSON

CANARIUM BOOKS
ANN ARBOR, MARFA, IOWA CITY

SPONSORED BY
THE HELEN ZELL WRITERS' PROGRAM
AT THE UNIVERSITY OF MICHIGAN

THE GREAT MEDIEVAL YELLOWS

Canarium Books
Ann Arbor, Marfa, Iowa City
www.canarium.org

The editors gratefully acknowledge the
Helen Zell Writers' Program at the University of Michigan
for editorial assistance and generous support.

The author wishes to thank the editors of the journals in which
some of these poems first appeared: *Barrelhouse*, *Colorado Review*,
Iowa Review, *Kenyon Review*, *Lana Turner*, *LVNG*, and *Yalobusha*.
Deep thanks also to Robyn Schiff and to all at Canarium Books.

Cover photograph:
Sylvia Sharnoff, *Caloplaca* and *Acarospora* lichens

First Edition

Printed in the United States of America

ISBN 13: 978-0-9849471-8-8

To Everett and Gideon

CONTENTS

HIBERNAL   3

METALMARK   4

THE GARDEN   6

MEZZOTINT   8

SECRETIVE SOIL FAUNA   9

NOCTURNE   11

HEROIC PIGMENTS   12

EQUIVALENTS FOR A MEGALITH   13

BIG TECHNICAL   14

CRAFTING GLORIOUS HEDGES   15

DIGITATED LEMON   16

SIPHONOPHORE   17

FLUME   18

MAPPA MUNDI   19

STADDLES   20

INSULAR   22

VOICES AND WORDS   25

STROBILUS   26

MONOLOGUE   28

SACCADE   29

DRIED PANICLE   30

EIDOLON   32

HERBIER   33

FLORILEGIUM   34

EXHIBITION   35

MACHINAMENTA   36

INVASIVE   37

LITTLE FANTASY   39

BUDS   40

SPONGES, TRUE AND PROBABLE   42

CAUCASIAN WINGNUT   44

THE GREAT MEDIEVAL YELLOWS   49

FONDO D'ORO   50

FLAME HALL   51

PAINTED LADIES   52

THE MODEL HAND   53

GNOMON   54

COMMON COMFREY   55

BLACK REACTION   56

KUNSTKAMMER   58

PATTERNED GROUND   59

PARLIAMENT OF BIRDS   60

BIG BLUESTEM   61

LICHEN ASSOCIATION   62

SOUTH POLE   64

TURNED FIGURE   65

LITTLE BIGELOW   66

DURA MATER   71

The great medieval yellows, apart from gold, are orpiment and ochre, giallorino (probably usually massicot), mosaic gold, saffron, buckthorn, and weld.

—Daniel V. Thompson
The Materials and Techniques of Medieval Painting

THE GREAT MEDIEVAL YELLOWS

HIBERNAL

White-throated sparrow
throating out

spring the winter-
spring uptaken in

tracking the
moving subject moving off toward its lone
demolition compound

lumened limit
something human
reaching it

would not be reached
sprung, strung

subsumed
the forb in wielding what
it wields

deep rebounding strain
incurrent colors in the grain
broken through

one-two, one-two

let into
zones of a
strident radiation

METALMARK

Forbiddingly in
its primal vasculature, sunk
and tractable under
the sheath, the sussed buds,
the pitted way it
flourishes, finishing
off acute
strokes, congenital
cupped traces:
crude spots for
the furling wings,
the "metalmarks,"
webbed amid transposing
shocks beyond its circus—

>   clusters of it
>   feeding on oleanders
>   whatever is feeding
>   on the oleanders

Some kind of grub?
Halos clung to others
knifing in along the leaves
outright and spadelike
dusted with
stuffs the higher
chastenings emit.
Chiefly, what I am trying to learn,
luminous blacks,
"black dirties,"

all that has been scrapping itself here
amid the quarreling
reds and crimsons
wedged with art, hot
at the crosses—

THE GARDEN

Down in dusk
in the treads
the garden tends
into its own
untending, grown-
out scrupulous detail,
noxious deeds, the bowed
lustrous willows' busks
dealt to the ground, all
small detonations slung
to the pathways, none
but in the ruined
minuscule tells
what will be done:
the cedar disclosing long
from the inside out
in serial installments
in the midst of its piques
in apposite internal
rusts and browns:
it keeps to itself
bending back into
something else
staggeringly
kept up.
It can't be ended.
It must be ended in
mid-stride,
inside the husk,
in rucked or spiked

addenda: so
strains the eye
away from what
it wants: what
does it want?
what wants it?

MEZZOTINT

Open the book. Scan the artful
page that pins things up—the cryptic
bud working too to square the sense
of a syndicated order, its siphon
blossom flare stiff in the bract, an act
happens off that slender moil
you can't get through, sends streaks
through an arch distortion of
the core material—
bright green piping from
the "throat," "gut" where still
some question drives—can you live
within the resolution of
momentary detail, above it, propped
up over where the words hang
in rigid combines stitching through
their dark debris field and fail to discern—
how do I—turning back, the shagged
bark, felt hairs kissing down
the bracketed midrib grace of—
the crop the forced part?

SECRETIVE SOIL FAUNA

of the fungi
I have done

apart no crime
can come

sintered slew
mite and nematode

accosting in
the earliest makeshift

roots' most intimate
symbiosis

ever you crowd
the crowded shades

close to
blue mold spikes

granular
impacts of

the inexhaustible
crimp and sinus

plot just
how is it you

think you can
come in here and

scut the fatty mastics
off

the antagonies
the parsimonies

NOCTURNE

The stacks are bound
with crenellated piths
bredes and orchidlike
struts mapped to high
places that are virtual
complex scales or just
the only way to get anywhere
toward darkness made
of layers inchingly
proportional to
sound and disturbance
where gray breakers mold away
from their boundary blocks—
sleep, or the intrigues of
sleep in stepped-
off funneling flocks of
birds when you look down
like shoals glancing over
the vast reef subducting its traps—
to be close to
removed from
at once all unseen
touched-in
repentances how
are you anything
alive to such work

HEROIC PIGMENTS

Blue Alice blue cyan
akin to something
bristling on azurite
you have to add some
grit to the principal
substance the "carrier"
I think it's called
though I might never know
the true import
it comes out in
six or seven segregate heads
but in avoidance of
figures developing
much more eccentrically
spathe-like leaves
floating in stalls beneath
and down with that cheerfulness
in no particular
relation to you at its
centermost hesitant
to say anything even
to confess it
sticks in you
to even intimate it
must terribly be
what the art arched off from

EQUIVALENTS FOR A MEGALITH

Open the palm for its brazen cog.
Is it smaller than.
The exemplar.
Remember to take it.
Sanitarily though it groans and stings.
You gather the babe.
You wash and pare away.
The excess shoots.
In the stinking middle.
Plunder rigid with.
Varnish.
Almost contracted.
Stamens forcing up.
An intertexture.
Just the way the thing evolved.
Douce footbaths for.
The acrid ants.
In the entrusting folds.
We cannot know how far to the true.
One.
Is not a one.
But the figure furthered.
Up along its grooves.
The spires hatching on in.
Sheaves.
To make the measure of.

BIG TECHNICAL

rattling off
an old cottonwood
overhead and wind burring
in the bur oak
it all goes down in
flaming rods jittering stands
drawn and snagged

in surrounding steles
something truly vitreous
in the red crooks

big tick umbels
elaborating strewn and
shocking aster wields advancing
fritillary yellows clouded and
the spotted taupe-and-salmon-smeared

little droves
hovering shoulder level
you walk right in
and smell the burning material

rosy-studded stalwarts with the leaves almost
totally bitten out

CRAFTING GLORIOUS HEDGES

A day of work in your life
hearing and smelling, listening and feeling
all the ways about this you can feel
unaccountably, this and that, patternings
lost in the lawn, plantain, creeping
Charlie, something cursive in its climb
along the stones, stubbed endings
up in gaps, between being and persisting,
and modern fixtures in
the display meant to impart
an under-echeloned glow,
almost a gift of shadow, unreal, so
the strange absorbances
shame, misery, grief, horror, and death.

DIGITATED LEMON

Long-tapered tips, like
the tips of parsnips curling out,
pitted, sheepish portrait of
a "pregnant" sour orange,
"chimeric citron with excrescence,"
grave with exuberance.
I'm not comfortable.
Slugs of wood mimicking stone.
Stick bugs, caterpillars "in folio,"
that kind of thing
delivered in its hide, luciferous
borderline character, roughly
incriminated paleo-
type now innocent
again but seeming so
binged in the guard hairs
silvering, stammering.
Not really an "animal" I know
thoughts in terror grow
their diverse spandrels
but what was committed
in the margins of
enlarging parts
feared to be true
under-numberings of?
Look at the plain monstrosity.

SIPHONOPHORE

The chance tentacular array
would look like this—
several concentric catenations, lacings
or dense infringings on
sort of a rote
blue openwork, blue-penciled
puce, urn
from the side
little white squirts
collaring the cap
inverted and straining
the illusion of "rightness" of "oneness"
which end is
cut off from the prose
the motion
this way
goes we do not go
like this—like this—
fluxing and self-welding through
the stringent
element conceivably
rending, remembering
what you wanted it
to feel like
just look at you
button yourself back
the membranes held
down, in the dark
variorum.

FLUME

Just staying with it long enough
to know it is there

the difficult protruded edge

several inflorescences
seaming in the nestled head
a conversation going on in
gray, tin, tinsel, black, gray
and a row of fallen-outs
where the gangs fused
or were apprised of
something functionally just dropped off
I do not know what moves
the mechanisms—how

wide water still
precedes the burning
mountain torrent-
chutes through

the mind
sensing itself
a feat of

intricate barbarities told
in the waiting room

mindlessness

MAPPA MUNDI

Starlings burn their circuits in
three or four distinct
departures from
the trunk that was
straight driven up
against what was conjunct—
spars, semaphores
where the feet were
once implanted
determined the hands' slotted scope
the head's vast vesseling
in on itself
marveled out in
asymmetrical renderings of
the bones, vesicles, rivers
ballast grounds, dumps—
disk on which millipedes
skew and dinge—
protracted enterprise, you
have your pileated seed-crown
hashed wholly under
the trackless wind
how can, how can you
work with what is given you?

STADDLES

A spot for building up the stack.
Rich salt hays long ago pitched into
pinecone shape along the rounds
the river takes, "ring-racks," you can see
the stakes sunk in grass like teeth.
I think they're gone beneath the grasses now.
They stuck out there, before, distinctly,
like weird base parts of old
trees the earth took back to itself.
Something is slipping through the culverts
under the road, foaming from parcel
to parcel, astride the manned estrangements
into place.
Egrets show up in that low area
between the bank and railroad grade, stinging
the view with Dutch glints.
I'll make myself more plain.
The green resists its transoms.
Tall revolving shadows of the stacks.
I should be plain. It gets so hard
toward the starker intervals, where the grass is
no doubt changing, being brought down, at the sheath,
in casual whorls and thrusts
like waves the wind works into,
where the method has had to shift tones,
so close in shiving out the dark horizontals,
things or expressions, ulterior, in time,
so hard to engage with any decency.
All along the river there are stoppages
it broke off from, like the involving

furze, or so I imagine it
from above, spoiling out of itself
in gothic turns beyond the strain
that makes it want
to turn.

INSULAR

spending off into
the blue groins
rocks scouring
seaward of the dinted
wild rosehips and the timely
winter berries there among them
shingle all
we were bound to
aboriginal
underpinnings
tumbling up the steep
slake stringing
flailed skirmishes
always redoubling
never not
undoing
things done
—knotted, weedy, woolly, plastic
into the turns
the volvelle pins
the inter-chambered
ambered organs on
the intake furls
at rest in prime
outgoing you would
have to make
yourself stop

VOICES AND WORDS

Mist hitched in the thorn
The dodder cast its veil
Winter made return
Stemming the low sprawl
The harbinger's weed
I sought, I don't need

Whatever slipped its bed
Up through the buried shaft
Was bolder for the rude
Degree again of halved
Stone, I thought, bring
It back gruff

Degrading, what was flung
From the sun, scroll
In the least tongue
Which does unbind, fool
Floating, hung
I'll live my life on

STROBILUS

In ancient forms the forms are free
to intersect in pointed parts
so roadside parts are charms, prisms
to handle them is

Pull the shafts apart, then
finger-pink the segment-ends
back over the spurred tips, pinch
the sockets in a sense undoing

What just temporarily did
dismantle them, anyway, plants
should look like parts pursued in books
not to provoke

From the flickering article
needlelike scores of thatching frond
extruders, but, fine-tooled
microplasts bearing true immortal

Fungus-foxed resemblances
of what becomes the part I
thought would become
more, to attract the receptors to

Organ-pleat motif, mastery
tracked in rich grisailling baffled
basic formfuls of
genuine means to scuff skin

Scuff the skin.
Make it weep.
Feed the quaking spiral through.
Be fruitful. Be crenulated with want.

MONOLOGUE

It seemed the thing was juster
with its angles driven keener
giving depth and variation
to incising swallows black
along the traplines, slubs
in kinds of silk bent to
the spine, rounded, debossed
so I made the shadows, there
was room to mine the dry distracted
areas of sweet astride
the stark waiting to split the seasoned
cortex over-ridging the packed
flesh, the ruffed flesh marled
the bole, it was not flesh that glowed
off somewhat else but a dark mass
before the nineteenth century, though
I fell upon the work encumbered
as I was in verging snow
in a way of seeing through the stranded
vaults offwards, from the oak
the double-banded tucked and sheening
thing, world, withal
its stencil-webbed matters passing there.

SACCADE

In the photosensitive ground
my vision sleeps, stalked in love
and dread, in the metaphorical
fund we would be chemically
composed in, a simple order scanning
shoots moving whiplike overhead,
tripwire threads sprung from the least
constant, but to fix the sliding
sense, cluster-feeding subjects, things
we do on the retinal trap, still
we do them darker for the fovea
mills inside its nest, small
harlequin shark the eye bequeaths
somehow stranger to itself
astride the compassing mouth,
tensile glues, the mailed
shimmed enameling traveling to snap
the snap-strike future of its view, what
I feared, tinged, dissolved.

DRIED PANICLE

many intervals
dispersing

crossing
bringing
thought of

spring
jades sullen

undergunnings
along the sealed-

up glister-ground
ruggedness a fendedness

striking both, failure and our
feature, into

siege, externally,
if you look at them

are they ever
really

knapped
almost inward
bound

about the red shaft

I agree
"slit gatherings"

EIDOLON

Ivory under-throats just
rust-violet
you can see
for the mean
interceptions, pinged, pierced
several stringers, novelty
acts, high-borne displacements
puncturing an out-carpeting
theorem, not the same weight,
not the same specimen at all and
some get confused,
rough-laden, implicating
who holds contagion
where the face was
a blurred orb in-whirling
comes back at you
built out of paper or fruit
or passes of the calico
whole in which you must deal
shroud within shroud
for things scarcely
contain you.

HERBIER

And quiet strangely
struggled into, move around
to see where it has fit, then
can't it? Turning up a truculent
part—*Viola odorata*—you haven't
understood it as a symmetry, quite
the opposite, the funged leaf floats
and scrolls from its base, and finer
near the petal head, almost double-
tubular, an outride stem
rooted to
the rule of the plate, yet
possible
to find going into
an aperture something
slenderer than—stay with me
little textual interval
stabbed with a stem
ghost-stem, scrying under
the packed and fibrous scales
composing the "cone."
The leaves are cordate and the bud,
the bud taken sideways is
a toy blue—viola, *agréable*—
bowed free but being still
for the subtler hand that made thee
no one made thee

FLORILEGIUM

The double peony
doubling still its still
surround, the honeysuckle's
"rococo sinuosities" doing
their dippings into
shades a close rejoinder to
backward tugs in
petit-point sheaths all
the false conductions
wild importations going on
in deep shade under
the flailed honeysuckle
boring through the loose slats
sounds like a drone
in phased
containments the artless
interest solitary
traced you could say
artlessly of
an "art"
that holds in place
hairstreak on
sheer tusk of mauve
delphinium
artless
brute appointment.

EXHIBITION

And where would you have put
The imaginary annelid if not in the comic
Near-embrace of the black lacquered scorpion
All in the glow of the bowl of a sulfur
Yellow tulip whose stem promptly ends
Implying a surface, strange, vertical-slatted
Shadow "under" the upturned filbert
Cups as if they rest in a shallow niche
Overhung with roman capital script proceeding
In reverse, the descending lengths of some
Of the ascenders is perverse, as
Twin horns of the larkspurs just
A shade away from the faintly rusting
Tulip head they curve to adorn are, the worm
Has "horns" too, confusing the tools
The arms brandish that would draw it
Viciously, very pointedly, toward the mouth?

MACHINAMENTA

That they resemble may be
that they have known
most intimately
bilobed and rubbed from
the beds, erstwhile
flesh compressions
olivish, tilting, etched
with vermilion, translucent
windowlike corneal
forms, stones
at the ciliate plates
sometimes stones
of the mind turn
up in the variant
cumbent, recumbent
vermiculite dark
exerting its surfaces
why don't you ever
extend yourself
why don't
you try to
make yourself somehow
extend yourself
endless foraging
feverine shits out its mince
counterparts for
the pinned-in
tractable counterparts for the
morbid endurances.

INVASIVE

Another path
another purpling
path path
rush against
gray stone
what is gray
purpling
reddish fuzzed
barrowed off
some poor
ditch
opening—
stone you are
fitted to
wilding cracks in
complex studded
blends spontaneous
inter-edged networks
nimbly
variegating
rush rushed
disjointed up ahead
upon entering
from the ocular point
behind seen and
shored forward through—
through-wiring—but
the breaks in metrics
essentially are

underfoot
and of the foot
root rushed onward

LITTLE FANTASY

I am not having it, the habit of it, what
raked me through
the privet twigs brushed and tugged
the rutilant hedge, a hedging of, birds
hurled toward me, just to the
point of me—
was it you who veered
from me, from the fleet point—
was it even where I was when
dealt the blurring emblem of its crown,
shocked, spiraled, crimson-brown "blossoms"
more like stamped copper bosses
on the brown
almost
unanswerable
graduating gloss about this town
flagrant yellow-greens against
that too-intense blue, I'll leave it inside
the sense of what I saw
where the limbs were taken down—ovals—
from a marvelous height.

BUDS

torsions of, ruby
spiked colonies under
the peonies
meatier than
imagined points turned up
at the specializing
ends even where you find
the need to move on
more of a reddish
pink toward the terminals
flocking and bobbling
several gnarled shots
tall for a crabapple
moreover
you cannot know
how one gives on another
"impressions of" keen
counter-faction
indicators of
something forfeiting deeply
forfeited for
a round incoming
interrupted bucks
the whole fringe
attending it
seems I've seen that all
before it shambles down
some vague node
messing it, though
quite a unity

undergirds the sharp
chartreuse moments
done alone

SPONGES, TRUE AND PROBABLE

Calcareous crinoline
what's unwound in

gone soft parts
probably didn't give enough

I want to make up
my love's lover's leaf

of white scurf
possibly only

for a while
subtended the primordial

bud it was
slunk just before

crystallized bibbings off
the flawed stalk

bad at this because
it's hard to be

"in it" they say
for any stay

astride the clarifying
ruddy scrolling spicule-sprigging

thing
splendidest bastion

CAUCASIAN WINGNUT

Or could it bear some likeness to
the heroine hand going, going for
the catch—
roving toward the dark vent
total encompassing yet
out-bounded by the sense
one must extend, grasp
the pin
from its rusted bed
arch void or pocked
forest glass deepening its task
of openness flung
forcibly shoved
against its hinges
heaving in on
shims, inanimate
ledge stuff, vegetable-
tinted emblems of
the frame coped inside its bay
rich with cellulose-
threaded spectral detail
with some interior still
for a small Egyptian frond
tree, tissue trace incised in stone
a fern progenitor
unknittable in turn
to the tender cystic gypsum-
haired polypodium—
or, just my own flawed entrapments
jamming through

the studded plates—
hand that compels
the other hand
tipped with sporing cones
strewed chert points the peregrine
hand floats and courses
pivots and juts
the self extreme where
starlight combs its secrets into
the picture therein which
builds its wych elms off
what sleeps in the goddamned
ground it came
vernacular rough cut
tilting from
the chastened ground
it spun from
outer space
with each inverse
imago meets its cursed
luminous edge.

THE GREAT MEDIEVAL YELLOWS

Massicot mosaic gold
saffron buckthorn weld—
how to get your gilding on
it will not take part in
ruination of the blue.
Or drubbing through the known earths
in preparation for
the flesh
would it be upheld,
its chalcedony.
What you are here for
your ardent understanding of
what self in many
moving faculties
that make it so like self—
suckers through the roots of
the undulant woad
it has been living
all along
oxidizing under the topic
brilliance, hematite, lime white,
a little pinch in the dish
you have only to wait for it.

.

FONDO D'ORO

But how can it be
again, after the long
year, this brilliant,
mystifying and yellowish
radishy pink, staining
its lobe, coppling its tree,
tincturing its street?
Let the world go
where it can keep
in the gray codes
unconstructed,
the wire-rigid perplexities
of the seminal acts,
subtle norms of the softer
resiliences, let
the thing go so secretly
charged, dazzling
stints, grim pinpoints,
bald and blossoming
dark incendiary course.

FLAME HALL

Given the ground opens just for a moment
glinting up its smither-weights of glass
the several octahedral relief modes have composed
dense, twilled variations ridden with colorants—
so endue the powers with undue art—
lazurites, the onion-green laterally mending
prase, oh, humble copper nubbling
under tricks, I only want you to move
the parts that will move, given the crude thing
through you, bleak with gold, fuscous and
constellating, given the ground
opens into
something,
not, unreal—or,
infamous
strange
derivatives.

PAINTED LADIES

Blood-orange-tracked against the netting
where the cut carnations act
in funnel groups the sliced-
open Clementine
stiffening along the spokes
and special bramble in
the sun's phase when it comes
they block their wings
clinging and hingeing
that what has stepped inside itself off
from itself
splints out of
barely
pinned again
in the sense of
beheld—trashed
sumps of paper
towel blossom sweetened often.

THE MODEL HAND

The somewhat off-sized
illuminated "I"
pedals its gold kerns
at the edge of
the (unknown?) text, which gives
if you will
from its tweediness
to retiform wings
of a dragonfly tipped in below
stiff-haired, protracted
calamine blue and sectored
hemimorphite pilaster to—
the wings in congress—
arcs of the common
pear leaf and half-pried
bud of the wastrel carnation.
It was opposed to the tight blossom
end that the stem apparently
snaked to the woodier
stem, it has been my misfortune—
sheltered things so
supernaturally
in confidence with
what I was
trying to pay attention to—

GNOMON

Slow chains of the richening
awkward outward
growth and change
to have lived
jointedly through
the fluid binding stills of old
sandstone—
fish, fishy fans, budded
loaflike discoids and
the otherwise
"gauche spiral in space"
something to have seen yourself
whether altered
backward
steeply borne
cobbled under waves
of white sediment—
split, botched, off
the strict integral
line of
thought
prone to—

COMMON COMFREY

What you have of the head, a fanned candelabrum,
rustic cymes twisted under themselves,
the hairiness, a clicking in the bones, the bones
make strange, implacable signets of
the parted parts.
Between the stalks and the buds,
behind their "arrangement," the dark
graining muted tumid ground.
Will I be forgiven?
And isn't this a madness you can see
adhered to its plan, patterns in
gold, basalt, kermes, cadmium, and steel?

BLACK REACTION

Silver chromate salts
channeling chinked
along the hanging fig
cutouts of the nerves—
"neuroglia," bulbings of—
what I'm scanning as
the sum of someone's
scrupulous jitter-lines
tendered "from nature,"
the fine mink hairs
arborescing, penetrating
almost starlike
ticks embedded, or
dwarf tubers, beets
with roots unlikely
raveling from both ends
sheared off at the "crown,"
the "sheath," whatever
it is, it is the oblong
languid shapes
pending dark
inter-netted surfaces
delicate solder acts
that would unfold
across micrometers—
hemi-micrometers—
not to be commanded to
the eye itself but
in the never-cresting
conduct of the eye out of

the shadowing webs
in relation to
whose stultified end
we would not abandon
our hope and exact prey.

KUNSTKAMMER

Loose flotillas of snow in
dark junipers buttoned up
and down the joint stalks
round and round spalled
willed and will-less of one
equilibrium met in reasoned parts
teased together to uphold
certain routes to the windlass
so to let go of what was
fledged and shaped to the foot
coming through brutally
fashioned passages round
we tautened out our screen
challenging the neutral
tones to keep their ground
disturbing in our wake the leaves
the spelts culled squibs of
bond clinging along the filament
round to the stark
edge which had no horizon
but the snag spruce the black-
inscribing biomes where you comb
for a place to stand
in the open sounding
off the blown exposures
florid rimes.

PATTERNED GROUND

The cushion plants warp
in bands down slope
with the swift
ice-out with the fell's
defining freshets
tenderly by
the roots urged
against retainment—
to "move" to "grow"
endeared to one place
a shuck at the base
fundamentally
serves
I'll pay you
something
anything
that which I owe
for that which has been
here russeting
off the dark rock
down a vast
toothed
regularity.

PARLIAMENT OF BIRDS

The tree is rendered fit for them just so

Attendant branches spaced apart in a plane

Do not overslip the tinted wings, the sing-

Ularly curving beaks, vents and peppered

Corsets sporting the town illusion we

Have come to abide in all the soldier-colored

Tufts competing in the abstruse copper

Rules so each is dutiful through its own

Enveloping hand-pixeled scape each bird

Is perfect though the child would never select

It which was not that

One with the tail a crazy squamous symbol

Hard to match from the cramped notes

Were they inclined to picket into the shadowy

General blinking mid-unfastening half-

Suspended from some demi-whorl or drift of

Barely sutured beech's skin if

They could survive this.

BIG BLUESTEM

They reach but do not hold serrate sounds
Down, on the disturbances, yeasting, mustering,
Cold April air tunneling over them,
The dominant dentation with which the bluestem
Moved uncountered, so took the mid-
Slope back, in "true" association is
The word not conducted like that grass
From stiff points sunken in, the burrowed
Word, tillering, tillering, the word itself
Trends back from itself, flecked culm
Spending freely what it earned from its long
Stand in the sun, its long-borne bow under the wind.

LICHEN ASSOCIATION

Something is speaking
in the language of
orange areoles
in the manner of
black plaques and
silvery gritted miniature
British soldiers or
are they spiders' flagons
one must imagine
the thrill and eclipse both
when something is delivered
in the tenor of
velvet tripes trenching
the squalid rock
things that blanch over it
messages rampant
restrictiveness hey
you have to listen
in the impress between
passages thatched of
biogeochemical
realities something is
pitching in an effort to
extenuate to somehow
expand on the tangible
synthesis "rare and
hardly gotten"
don't you realize
the implications of
mind-blowing bare

horizontals where
someone always
vanishing trespassing
is.

SOUTH POLE

the stakes become
a strict archipelago
from the known
scudded-over primary
plot but was I
there was what I saw
seabirds on
the long ice
runway someone said
above the glitter
ruts rigorously
heaved and forked twin
ensigns of
a silent stemming
peripheral real
off the far end
where the plane went down
then was laid in
with snow
you could crawl through
and just make out the gloomed
panels no one died
what will be done
the brittle rifts and windows
vents cuts
metallic stranded flock
dumps depositories yields strewments

TURNED FIGURE

All the bead, all the bore
to send it down, you haven't lived

dispassionately, only
touched on, the living commune

sewage rut, in distributed
acts and executions, I

didn't know you, friend
vestibular, strutted

through the mist material, brave
simplex, the whole job

shifts in the willows'
plaids, pounced against the soot-

instructed background wall, the "grotto"
of the "heart"

the tumbled heart.

LITTLE BIGELOW

Room around it
down the slabs
tumbled "tubs"
cracked blasts
the bossed stones
replicating
sharper stones
I would not ask for
ramping wild off
stalled
things
they could be
who but curbs
tarns
tampers
shagged beaks
pent assemblages
mid-wield but
are these the things
I want to ring
to hold

You can replace a word
with other words
but not its transverse
slide moving stiff, diagonal
upward, up until
the path reverts
to basement stone
stacked
torquing through
the spruce space
the sense of it
darker switching
prickling, patching, scrubbed
a sumptuous
seepage just
under what
constitutes—
I can hardly see
nearing me—
the leveling plenitude—

In this high intimacy
the mountain asks
through formulating
joists its reserves
its floats its
overlooks—here,
you get those blowsy clouds
blotting the baize,
some are really moving,
streaming so,
eventually though
they reach some forced
conclusion, perfectly
registered, cold, and disappear—
isn't it amazing—
barely
having gotten past
that stringency

The "horns" are for hammering
tin for the toes
boots for the corpse
congruent, I
have not tired yet
the mountain shaves
itself down
meat and metal have met
to the slanting bone—
tender shadbush bones—
and in kind
the mind scuffs after

Nothing serves the obdurate
top, stolid, buzzing
thunderous above
strict pediments. No
it's neither that, nor this, it is not
even likenable, certainly
smirched with pits
all over its surface—
from which to garner more surface?
Neither likely in my lifetime
is the underlying source
of an underlying loss—primal
redactedness—chance
sort for the chanced-
upon balking sub-rock,
broken febrile greens,
the combat greens, hunters within
the lumbering shapes of the hunt.
It is something.
To stand on it toppling.
Having almost never been here.

DURA MATER

Was impeded
Could not bring myself
To show/care outwardly
Pedimented
You were difficult
To attend
You had a way of
Putting me off
I would be put off
To the small ends
Even when I knew you
Needed

Are there worlds within
Dusk sublunars within
The volute matters
That I should comfort you
Still
In other words if
In some other amplitude
I could present to you
A salver holding tools
Of my own making—
If I could make them—
From the thorns
And common cleavages
Along the vivid
Castellated
Forms of stone-
Dissolving refuse and the firs

Dispensed stunting through
The firs within
Cold incursions
Pin-pricked stoma so
Immense strobed parietals
Hold the wind?

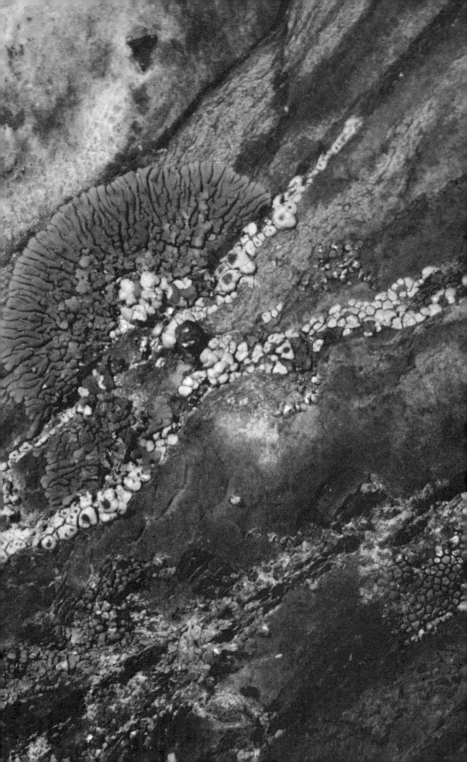